First World War
and Army of Occupation
War Diary
France, Belgium and Germany

17 DIVISION
Divisional Troops
Royal Army Medical Corps
Divisional Field Ambulance Workshop Unit
15 June 1915 - 2 April 1916

WO95/1997/1

The Naval & Military Press Ltd
www.nmarchive.com
Published in association with The National Archives

Published by

The Naval & Military Press Ltd

Unit 10 Ridgewood Industrial Park,

Uckfield, East Sussex,

TN22 5QE England

Tel: +44 (0) 1825 749494

www.naval-military-press.com

www.nmarchive.com

This diary has been reprinted in facsimile from the original. Any imperfections are inevitably reproduced and the quality may fall short of modern type and cartographic standards.

© Crown Copyright

Images reproduced by permission of The National Archives, London, England, 2015.

Contents

Document type	Place/Title	Date From	Date To
Heading	WO95/1997/1		
Heading	17th Division 17th F.A. Workshop Unit Jun 1915-mar 1916		
Heading	17th Ambulance Work Shop Unit Vol: I June To July 1915		
War Diary	Neuf Chatel	18/07/1915	18/07/1915
War Diary	Abbeville	19/07/1915	19/07/1915
War Diary	St Omer	23/07/1915	25/07/1915
War Diary	Bueschepe	25/07/1915	30/07/1915
Heading	War Diary Of 17th Division Field Ambulance Of Work Shop Line From:- June 15th 1915 to July 31st 1915		
War Diary	Grove Park R.D	15/06/1915	15/06/1915
War Diary	Basingstoke	16/06/1915	16/06/1915
War Diary	Bulford	11/07/1915	11/07/1915
War Diary	Bath	12/07/1915	12/07/1915
War Diary	Avonmouth	12/07/1915	13/07/1915
War Diary	Southampton	13/07/1915	13/07/1915
War Diary	Roven	14/07/1915	17/07/1915
Heading	17th F.A.W.U. Vol 2 Aug 15 Aug 1916		
Heading	War Diary of 17th Div Field Ambulance & Workshop Unit From Aug 1st To Aug 31st 1913 Vol 2		
War Diary	Boeschepe	12/08/1915	12/08/1915
War Diary	Reninghelst	31/08/1915	31/08/1915
Heading	17th F.A.W.U. Vol 3 Sept 15 Oct 15		
Heading	War Diary Of 17th Division Field Ambulance Workshop Unit from Sept 1st To Sept 30 1913 Vol 3		
War Diary	Reninghelst	01/09/1915	30/09/1915
Heading	War Diary Of 17th Div Field Ambulance Workshop Unit From Oct 1st Oct 31st 1915 Vol 5		
War Diary	Reninghelst	06/10/1915	29/10/1915
Heading	17th F.A.W.U. Vol: 4 Oct 1915		
Heading	War Diary Of 17th Div A.W.U. From Oct 1st to Oct 31st 1915		
War Diary	Reninghelst Eecke	06/10/1915	29/10/1915
Heading	17th Division 17th F.A.W. Vol 5 Nov 15		
Heading	War Diary Of 17th Div F.A.W.U. From Nov 1st to Nov 30th 1915		
War Diary	Poperinghe	01/11/1915	27/11/1915
Heading	17th F.A.W.U. Vol 6 Dec 1915		
Heading	War Diary Of 17th Div F.A.W.U. From Dec 1st to Dec 31st 1915		
War Diary	Poperinghe	02/12/1915	31/12/1915
Heading	17th F.A.W.U Vol 7 Jan 1916		
Heading	War Diary Of 17th Div F.A.W.U. From 1-1-16 to 31-1-16		
War Diary	Poperinghe	06/01/1916	31/01/1916
Heading	War Diary Of 17th Div F.A.W.U. From Feb 1st to Feb 29th 1916 Vol 8		
War Diary	Eperlecques	06/02/1916	08/02/1916
War Diary	Bueschepe	08/02/1916	29/02/1916

War Diary	Bueschepe	28/02/1916	28/02/1916
War Diary	Bueschepe	06/02/1916	06/02/1916
Heading	War Diary Of 17th Div F.A.W.U. From March 1st to March 30 1916		
War Diary	Armentiere	02/04/1916	02/04/1916

17TH DIVISION

17TH F.A. WORKSHOP UNIT

JUN 1915-MAR 1916

17TH DIVISION

121/6300

17th Australian Workshops Unit

Vol. I

June 1915
July 15
Nov '16

WAR DIARY
or
INTELLIGENCE SUMMARY

Army Form C. 2118.

(Erase heading not required.)

Instructions regarding War Diaries and Intelligence Summaries are contained in F. S. Regs., Part II. and the Staff Manual respectively. Title pages will be prepared in manuscript.

Place	Date	Hour	Summary of Events and Information	Remarks and references to Appendices
Hemel Hempstead	18/7/15	9.30 AM	Left Head-Qtrs. Arrived Abbeville 4.30 PM.	
Abbeville	19/7/15	9.30 AM	Left Abbeville. Arrived St Omer 6.0 PM.	O.C. 17th Div: F.A.W.U. Lieut: [signature]
St Omer	23/7/15	4.0 pm	Storage 14 x 42 from DDRAMS to report personally at 17th Div. HQ without delay	
"	"	8.30 pm	Stables taken in hand by DADMS. Cars to me.	
"	24/7/15	10.30 AM	From DADMS heard nothing eqlist at meet for Div to HQ 17th Div:	
"	"	11.15 pm	Seng: Reeve left for 17th Div HQ for instructions.	
"	24/7/15	9.30 pm	Orders from DADMS to proceed to Steenwerck & report to ADMS 17th Div on 25.7.15	
"	25/7/15	10.0 AM	left St Omer	
Poperinghe	"	1.15 pm	Arrived Steenwerck & found Division had left for Reninghelst; phoned to DDMS that unit was arrived by ADMS & proceed to Boeschepe & remain till further orders.	
"	"	3.30 pm	arrived Boeschepe.	
"	"	6.30 pm	handed over 53rd F.A. section to O.C. F.53. F.A.	
"	"	7.30 pm	handed over 52nd F.A. section to O.C. F.52. F.A. at Reninghelst.	
Boeschepe	28.7.15	4.0 pm	handed over 61st F.A. section to O.C. F.51st F.A. at Reninghelst.	
"	28.7.15	4.30 pm	Saw A.D.O at Reninghelst & made arrangements for Returning.	
"	30.7.15		Instructions from D.D.G.T. + 2nd Army HQ to report all new figures htm.ref: 7/2040/15.	

Confidential.

War Diary of:-

14th Divisional Field Ambulance Workshop Unit.

From:- June 15th 1915.   To:- July 31st 1915.

[signature] Lieut:
O.O. 17th Div: F.A.W.U.
4.8.15

Army Form C. 2118.

WAR DIARY
or
INTELLIGENCE SUMMARY.
(Erase heading not required.)

Place	Date	Hour	Summary of Events and Information	Remarks and references to Appendices
Grove Park R.D.	15/6/15	—	Instructions from Orderly Room Grove Park Reserve Depot to proceed to Bulford and report to O.C. M.T. Depot.	
— do —	"	12.30 pm	Left Grove Park with unit for Bulford; arrived Basingstoke 6.30 pm and parked lorries in Thorneycroft's yard for the night.	
Basingstoke	16/6/15	10. am	Left Basingstoke for Bulford. Arrived Bulford 2 pm same day.	
Bulford	11/7/15	10 AM	Left Bulford with unit for Avonmouth. Arrived Clarendon nr Bath 2.30 PM and parked Ambulances for the night.	
Bath	12/7/15	9.30 AM	Left Bath with unit arrived Avonmouth 12 noon.	
Avonmouth	12/7/15	5 PM	Embarked Ambulances & lorries with 12 N.C.O's. men 5 PM	
Avonmouth	13/7/15	7.30 AM	C.O. and 59 N.C.O's & men entrained 7.30 AM for Southampton	
Southampton	13/7/15		Arrived 12 noon, embarked per S.S. Minneiah 5 PM	
Rouen	14/7/15	5.20 PM	Arrived Rouen.	
Rouen	16/7/15		Ambulances arrived per S.S. Lala.	
Rouen	19/7/15	10 AM	Three heavy lorries arrived by road from Havre	
Rouen	19/7/15	2 PM	Received movement orders	
Rouen	19/7/15	3 PM	Left Rouen; Arrived Treuy Châtel 7.30 PM	

121/7514

1st Revision

17th F.A.W.U.
Vol 2

Aug 15

Confidential.

War Diary
of:-
14th Divisional Ambulance & Motor Ambulance

from August 1st to August 31st 1913

(Vol. 2)

Army Form C. 211

WAR DIARY
or
INTELLIGENCE SUMMARY.
(*Erase heading not required.*)

Instructions regarding War Diaries and Intelligence Summaries are contained in F. S. Regs., Part II. and the Staff Manual respectively. Title pages will be prepared in manuscript.

Place	Date	Hour	Summary of Events and Information	Remarks and references to Appendices
Borrehope	12.8.15	9.15 am.	Received instrns from OC 5B⁰ + Amb. to proceed to Reninghelst + be attached to 51st + Amb.	3/ O.C. 17th Div: F.A. [signature]
	"	2.30pm.	left Borrehope for Reninghelst.	
Reninghelst	"	4.30.	arrived Reninghelst + attached to 51st + Amb & Took up position G.34a3.8.	
	31.8.15		Changed position took up position G33a8.2	

S/12/7517

17th F.A.W.U.
Vol 3
Sept 15

Confidential.

Mesopotamy
&c.
14th Div: Field Ambulance to establishment

from Sept 1st to Sept 30th 1917

(vol. 4) 3

WAR DIARY
or
INTELLIGENCE SUMMARY.

Army Form C. 2118.

Place	Date	Hour	Summary of Events and Information	Remarks and references to Appendices
Reninghelst	1st to 30th Sept. 1915		position G.33.a.B.2 throughout. Nil of importance to record.	

(signature) — Lieut:
O.C. 17th Div: F.A.W.U.

Confidential.

Maintaining
of
Div: tens Ambulance Workshop Unit.

from Oct 1st to Oct 31st 1915

(Infirs)

WAR DIARY
or
INTELLIGENCE SUMMARY.

(Erase heading not required.)

Army Form C. 2118

Place	Date	Hour	Summary of Events and Information	Remarks and references to Appendices
Reninghelst	6.10.15	9.0 pm	left Reninghelst for Eecke.	Lieut. [signature] O.O. 17th Div: F.A.W.U.
Eecke	"	11.30 pm	took up new position Q 20 c 8.8.	
"	17.10.15	2.30 p	Staff Sergeant E.W.J) Mc Gibbon returned to M.T. Depot. Base attached to 52 D.T. Amb.	
"	21.10.15		left Eecke + took up position near Poperinghe L 23 A 2.5	
"	22.10.15	9.45 pm	Staff Sergeant Thos Mr/1865 returned to unit.	
	29. x. 15			

17ᵗʰ Jany.
Vol: 4

War Diary
of
175th Bde. + A.M.C.
from Oct 1st to Oct 31st 1915

BMC Rose
Confidential.

Army Form C. 2118.

15 KW + A.W.U.

WAR DIARY
or
INTELLIGENCE SUMMARY.
(Erase heading not required.)

Instructions regarding War Diaries and Intelligence Summaries are contained in F. S. Regs., Part II. and the Staff Manual respectively. Title pages will be prepared in manuscript.

Place	Date	Hour	Summary of Events and Information	Remarks and references to Appendices
Remingelst	6.10.15	9.0 pm	15/ RENINGHELST to EECKE	
EECKE		1.30 pm	Took up new position R 20 e 8.8.	
"	17.10.15		Staff Surgeon LLOYD. C.A. MS/1603 attached to M.T. dept. at Base	Lieut: [signature] O.C. 17th Div: F.A.W.U.
"	21.10.15		my Unit attached to 52 D.T. Ambulance.	
"	22.10.15		15/ EECKE + Forke up position L 2 3 a 2.5	
"	29.10.15		Staff Surgeon LLOYD. C.A. MS/1603 returned to unit.	

D/7605

F F McKwin

17th F.A.W.V.
Vol 5

Nov. 15

K

Nov 1915

Confidential

Wantsing
of
By Detain + A.W.C
to Nov. 30th 1916

[signature]

WAR DIARY
or
INTELLIGENCE SUMMARY.

(Erase heading not required.)

Army Form C. 2118

Place	Date	Hour	Summary of Events and Information	Remarks and references to Appendices
Poperinghe	1-11-15	—	position still L.23.a.2.5.	
—	20-11-15		Returned 51st F. Amb: Dranoutre Ambulance (C.3) to G.H.Q. no. 15110.	
—	21-11-15		Collected Dranoutre Ambulance 14485 for 51st F. Amb: from II Army Troop Supply Co.	
—	22-11-15		Returned 52nd F. Amb Dranoutre Ambulance (B.3) HS. JTR N° 15105.	
—	22-11-15		" 53rd " " (A.5) " ROUEN N° 15164	
—	27-11-15		Received 2 Wolseley Ambulances from II ~ Army Troop Supply Col — for 52nd + 53rd Amb. (M.T.68) (N° 41h)	Lieut: [signature] O.C. 17th Div: F.A.W.U.

17th F.a.w.u.
vol 6

121/7894

14th F.A.

Dec 1915

Confidential.

Was firm in
his refusing to
give it to
him from 26.10.12 – 1913.

WAR DIARY
or
INTELLIGENCE SUMMARY.

Army Form C. 2118.

(Erase heading not required.)

Instructions regarding War Diaries and Intelligence Summaries are contained in F. S. Regs., Part II. and the Staff Manual respectively. Title pages will be prepared in manuscript.

Place	Date	Hour	Summary of Events and Information	Remarks and references to Appendices
Poperinghe	2.12.15		Received 1. Siddeley Deasy Ambulance 15343 for 51st F. Amb. from 2nd Army Trnsp. & M.T. Co.	O.O. 17th Div: F.A.W.U.
"	3.12.15		Returned 51st F. Amb. Isiville 15106 to 52nd F. Amb. Isiville 15 of S.M.T.R.	
	4.12.15		Received 1. Siddeley Deasy Amb: 15344 for 51st F. Amb. from 2nd Army Trnsp & M.T. Co.	
	7.12.15		Received 15345 for 52nd F. Amb. D°.	
	7.12.15 to 15.12.15		9 was on leave to England.	
	19.12.15		Returned to 3rd F. Amb. Talbots 15100 & 15102 to A.S.C. Repair Shops, Paris.	
	"		Received 2. Siddeley Deasy Amb: 15973 & 15348 for 53rd F. Amb. from 2nd Army Trnsp. & M.T. Co.	
	30.12.15		Received 1. Deasy Amb: 15974 & 1. Ford Amb: 9938 from 2nd Army Trnsp. & M.T. Co. to 52nd F. Amb;	
	31.12.15		Returned 1. Isiville Amb: 15105 & 1. Wolsley Amb: 8481. Wolseley Amb: 8481 from 52nd F. Amb. to 2nd Army Trnsp. & M.T. Co.	

17ᵗʰ F. a. s. u.
vol: 7

F

Jan 1916

WAR DIARY
or
INTELLIGENCE SUMMARY.

Army Form C. 2118.

Place	Date	Hour	Summary of Events and Information	Remarks and references to Appendices
6.1.16. 31.1.16	Midnight		Left L 23 a 2,5 and Took up position at Chateau de la Vicogne. Appendix no S.O. No. 2	
	16.1.16		9A.M. at EPPERLECQUES	
	16.1.16		Received from B- Army Transp Supply Col: WOLSELEY Amb: 9871. to 52 F. Amb. Handed on FORD Amb: 9482 from 52 F. Amb: to O.C. 50 Div: F.A.W.U.	

Lieut:
O.C. 17th Div: F.A.W.U.

17th F.A.W.U.
Vol. 8.

War Diary
of
17th Div: F.A.W.U.

Feb 1st to Feb 29th 1916.

[signature] Lieut:
O.O. 17th Div: F.A.W.U.

WAR DIARY
or
INTELLIGENCE SUMMARY.

(Erase heading not required.)

Army Form C. 2118.

Place	Date	Hour	Summary of Events and Information	Remarks and references to Appendices
Poperinghe	6.2.16		Evacuated sick to Amb. 15114 & 51st F.A. & to Amb.	Lieut: [signature] O.C. 17th Div: F.A.W.U.
"	8.2.16		Left Poperinghe	
Busseboom	8.2.16		Took up new position at Busseboom & attached to 53rd F. Amb: Evacuated position sheet 27. R9d9.8	
"	29.2.16		Still in same position	
"	28.2.16		Took over from 14th M.A.C. kit [Military Amb: Talbots Nº. 17239, 17240, 17241, 17242, 17243, & Lancia three car Saunders Amb. Nº. 15113, 17485, 18345, 9530, 1011.	
"	1.2.16		Staff Sergt: Mutimer F.LL. L/Cpl. O.A. evacuated to C.C.S. sick.	
"	"		Cmg. Sgt. N.T.J.E. J.N. appointed A/Staff Sergt. Mechanist in place of above N.C.O. Pte. Strathridge S. appointed A/Corporal in place of Sergt. G. Mutimer	

17 Div
F.A.W.U.
Vol. 9

COMMITTEE FOR THE
MEDICAL HISTORY OF THE WAR
Date

War Diary of:-
17½ Div. F.A.W.U.C.

from March 1st to March 31st 1916

Army Form C. 2118.

WAR DIARY
or
INTELLIGENCE SUMMARY.
(Erase heading not required.)

Instructions regarding War Diaries and Intelligence Summaries are contained in F. S. Regs., Part II. and the Staff Manual respectively. Title pages will be prepared in manuscript.

Place	Date	Hour	Summary of Events and Information	Remarks and references to Appendices
ARMENTIERES	2-4-16		+ A.W.U athletics, + personal transfers to O.C. 17/S Div Supply Col.	
	3-4-16		[signature] Lieut: O.C. 17th Div: F.A.W.U.	

www.ingramcontent.com/pod-product-compliance
Lightning Source LLC
Chambersburg PA
CBHW081502160426
43193CB00014B/2567